Britney
A Life in Music

Yep, She Did it Again!

Comeback Kid Who Never Left!

This is a FLAME TREE Book

FLAME TREE PUBLISHING
6 Melbray Mews
Fulham, London SW6 3NS
United Kingdom
www.flametreepublishing.com

First published 2022

22 24 26 25 23
1 3 5 7 9 8 6 4 2

ISBN: 978-1-83964-963-9
ebook ISBN: 978-1-83964-964-6

The cover image is by Jean Baptiste Lacroix/Stringer/WireImage
via Getty Images

A copy of the CIP data for this book is
available from the British Library.

Printed and bound in the UK by Clays Ltd, Elcograf S.p.A

Britney
A Life in Music

Yep, She Did it Again!
Comeback Kid Who Never Left!

Nadia Cohen

Malcolm Mackenzie
(Foreword)

UNOFFICIAL

FLAME TREE
PUBLISHING

Contents

Foreword

Ever since Britney Jean Spears swooshed down that school corridor and into our lives, we have been a little bit besotted. She arrived in 1999 while we were enjoying something of a pop renaissance - Backstreet Boys, Steps, Destiny's Child, *NSYNC - but she was the teen queen of the lot.

In the early 2010s, pop enjoyed another growth-spurt with the likes of Rihanna, Justin Bieber, Lady Gaga and Katy Perry, but guess what? Decades later, Britney was still up there with them, scoring worldwide hits with ease. In fact, demand for Britney has never waned. Simon Cowell paid her a reported $15 million to be a judge on US X-Factor and her residency at Las Vegas was the highest-grossing at the time.

The Britney we first fell in love with was a wholesome girl-next-door in pigtails, but our crush deepened as she found a fondness for red latex, double denim, dancing draped in a python and indicating the emergency exits. Her personal life has had more than its fair share of ups and downs, but somehow, through it all, her music has remained steady – a constant string of non-stop bops.

I finally met Britney on the campaign trail for her 2011 album *Femme Fatale* and she was lovely, but of course I can't help wonder if she really wanted to be there. At that time, Britney was navigating life under the strict supervision of a conservatorship she wanted nothing to do with. Her devoted fan-base campaigned for her freedom and ten years later, in 2021, the conservatorship came to an end. Now that Britney is finally 'free' I want her to continue to triumph and live the life she wants, but secretly I hope that includes making music that makes us all want to scream and shout: 'hit us, Britney, one more time!'

Malcolm Mackenzie

One More Time

'I really hoped and dreamed that all this would come to reality, but I really did not expect it to come so fast.'

Britney Spears

She may be one of the bestselling female recording artists of all time, with millions in the bank, two gorgeous children and a future that looks bright, but it has not been an easy journey for Britney Spears. But, despite the frequently public scandals, she's a survivor in a notoriously tough business. Her spectacularly

successful Las Vegas residency, Piece of Me, has cemented her place among the highest earning artists and she is worth at least a staggering $56 million.

Two Decades

With awards ranging from a Grammy to World's Sexiest Female, Britney has repeatedly risen to the top. Her career has already spanned two decades, and her time under the intense scrutiny of the media has been tough. Yet Britney continues to intrigue and entertain us as much now as the day she burst on to the scene in 1999.

Oh Baby

When the title track from Britney's first album, ...Baby One More Time, was released in January 1999, it was an instant sensation. It debuted at No. 1 not just on both sides of the Atlantic, but in 15 countries worldwide. Within a few months the album sold over 10 million copies and became the biggest-selling album ever by a teenage artist. The single sold 500,000 copies the first day it was released, and later received a Grammy nomination for Best Female Pop Vocal Performance. In Britain it became the fastest-selling single ever by a female artist, and remains the 25th most-successful song of all time in British chart history.

The now-famous video helped to fuel the phenomenon and she can take much of the credit for that. Her record label Jive originally wanted the video to be animated, but Britney had other ideas and suggested the raunchy schoolgirl look. It proved to be the first of many smart ideas.

'I don't want to be part of someone's Lolita thing.'

Britney Spears

Despite the raunchy pop persona, or perhaps because of it, Britney portrayed a squeaky clean image and declared she would remain a virgin until she married. However, she caused controversy in April of that year when she appeared on the cover of *Rolling Stone* wearing just a bra and shorts, sparking an outcry which led the American Family Association to urge 'God-loving Americans' to boycott stores selling Britney's albums.

Not A Quitter

A lot has changed for Britney since those early days. Two marriages and a very public mental breakdown seemed like the end of the world to her at the time, but since then she has reached new heights, with nine albums under her belt, a high-profile stint as a judge on *The X Factor USA*, and a record-breaking Las Vegas residency, with possibly another on the horizon.

But, among the successes, Britney still has to contend with difficulties along the way. Simon Cowell handpicked her for the role in 2012, with a reported salary of $15 million, making her the highest-paid talent show judge in TV history. However, she left after just one season, allegedly afraid that she was about to be fired for being 'boring'. Britney was brought in to boost ratings, but she was roundly criticized, not only for some of her fashion choices but also for fluffing lines and seeming disconnected from the contestants.

Ratings for the show continued to fall but Britney's comeback into the hearts of her fans was helped by her surprise decision to record a song with edgy producer will.i.am. He released 'Scream & Shout' on his album *#willpower* in December 2012, giving Britney's credibility a boost with a whole new audience.

'I've been through a lot, and there's a lot people don't know. Sometimes it can get lonely 'cause you don't open the gate. I'm stuck in this place, and I just cope every day.'

Britney Spears

Everyone Loves Britney

'I'm running on adrenaline and

the excitement – the electricity of

the audience.'

Britney Spears

ooking back, Britney had star quality from an early age. She performed in local shows and talent contests from the age of five, and when she was just eight, Britney enrolled at the Professional Performing Arts School after moving to New York with her mother. She was cast in several commercials and landed a small role in a Broadway show, but her big break came when she joined the Disney Channel's *The Mickey Mouse Club*.

Other future stars in the club were Christina Aguilera and, of course, Justin Timberlake. Although she was rejected the first time, at her second audition Britney was selected from 20,000 hopefuls, to the delight of residents in her hometown of Kentwood, Louisiana. Her parents Lynne and James have said they knew their daughter was always destined for show business.

She Has It All

From the first moment she tasted fame, there was no stopping Britney. Although the Mayor of Kentwood declared 24 April 1993 Britney Spears Day, she would never be a small-town girl again. After becoming a Mouseketeer, she signed with a prestigious Manhattan talent agency, Carson-Adler, and never looked back. Although *The Mickey Mouse Club* was cancelled and Britney had to briefly return home, she continued auditioning for record labels, and made a professional demo tape.

When music executives from Jive Records heard Britney sing in 1997, they instantly knew she had huge commercial appeal and signed her to a lucrative deal. Since she could sing, dance and looked great - known as the triple threat - they were determined not to let her slip through their fingers, so Britney was whisked off to a studio in Sweden with a team of producers and a vocal coach to start work on her first album. Although her career seemed to be taking off like a rocket, Britney's parents were so broke they filed for bankruptcy.

Schoolgirl Fantasies

When she returned from Sweden, Britney was launched on to the world, and her image was all about sex. Although a Jive executive suggested a cartoon video for her first song, showing Britney as a warrior princess superhero, she rejected the idea, thinking it wouldn't strike a chord with teenagers. It was the first time she had stuck up for herself, and it would certainly not be the last. Instead of Power Brit, she came up with the idea of a daydreaming schoolgirl. She tied her tight white shirt into a knot around her navel, and tied her hair into plaits, creating an iconic image. After appearing on the first *Total Request Live* on MTV wearing her saucy school uniform, she was immediately signed up to support the hottest boy band around, *NSYNC, on their tour.

Although she often reaffirmed her commitment to Christianity, some of her actions caused controversy, leading people to view her motives with suspicion. one example was the time she returned to Kentwood for a month's rest on doctor's orders, and emerged with much larger breasts. Although she insisted it was merely a 'growth spurt', former friends insisted she'd had surgery.

That was followed by the raunchy *Rolling Stone* photo shoot, accompanied by an interview headlined 'Is Britney Spears jailbait?' The following year, she performed a highly provocative dance routine at the MTV Awards wearing a flesh-coloured body suit. Amid all the controversy, she confirmed she was dating *NSYNC member Justin Timberlake.

Who Does She Love?

'Britney, to me, is an icon ...

she's our generation's Madonna

in terms of the way that she

changes as an artist, yet stays

true to the Britney we love.'

will.i.am on Britney Spears

Throughout Britney's career, critics and fans alike have compared her to Madonna. Like her professed idol, Britney has repeatedly reinvented herself and always managed to stay relevant and attract new audiences regardless of her personal struggles. Also like Madonna, her attempts at acting have been mocked, but Madonna herself admitted to being impressed by Britney.

In 2001, Madonna even seemed to adopt the role of the younger singer's mentor, when she openly defended her, saying. 'I want to do nothing but support her and praise her and wish her the best.' The older superstar started wearing T-shirts with Britney's name emblazoned on them, and dedicated her song 'What It Feels Like For A Girl' to Britney. Madonna's been generous with more than her support: she was seen wearing a $15,000 diamond necklace with an M hanging from it, and gave Britney a matching B.

Seal It With A Kiss

Madonna appeared to be a bit more than Britney's idol when the pair shocked the world with a passionate open-mouthed kiss at the MTV Video Music Awards in 2003.

For a performance of 'Like A Virgin', Britney took to the stage in a raunchy wedding dress and veil, before being joined on stage by Madonna in top hat and tails. While gyrating between Christina Aguilera and Britney, Madonna suddenly turned and started kissing Britney. Although the cameras focused on an uncomfortable-looking Justin Timberlake on the night, the photos went global and it was a show-stealing move, which finally shattered Britney's innocent image once and for all.

The outcry went around the world and both women, neither of whom had exactly been short of media interest during their careers, appeared delighted at being talked about like never before.

'I don't listen to anybody. I'm stubborn. But I do listen to Madonna. I wish I could be inside her head.'

Britney Spears

Keeping The Faith?

As a result of her friendship with Madonna, Britney became a follower of the Kabbalah religion. She even had various Hebrew symbols tattooed onto her neck as a sign of her devotion. It was after the annulment of her Las Vegas wedding to school friend Jason Alexander that she stopped attending her regular Baptist church and started showing an interest in this faith based on Judaism.

Although she was pictured carrying Kabbalah literature and wearing the followers' red string bracelet, her interest in the faith seemed to fade as fast as it began, and sources suggest her abandonment of Kabbalah was the reason she fell out with Madonna.

Britney has also named Michael Jackson and Whitney Houston as major sources of inspiration, and admitted she was star struck after meeting Janet Jackson. In turn, Britney has influenced a younger generation of pop stars including Nicki Minaj, Miley Cyrus and Katy Perry.

'Kabbalah helped me get rid of a lot of negative influences that were guiding me down the wrong path. There came a point when not even my family or advisers had the answers I needed.'

Britney Spears

I Wanna Be A Star

'When people are screaming

at shows... it's the most

flattering thing

there is and it just inspires

and motivates me to do a

better show.'

Britney Spears

Britney was born in 1981 in McComb, Mississippi
and raised in Kentwood with brother Bryan James

and younger sister Jamie Lynn. It was clear from an early age that she was destined to be a star, and was selected to perform a solo at her dance school's annual recital when she was just three. She made her stage debut at the age of five, singing 'What Child Is This?' at her kindergarten graduation, and went on to win local talent shows and gymnastics competitions before landing a series of acting roles in theatre productions and TV shows.

When she was eight, her schoolteacher mother Lynne took Britney to Atlanta to audition for the revival of *The Mickey Mouse Club*, but the casting director, Matt Casella, rejected her for being too young. He did, however, recommend her to a New York agent, Nancy Carson, who encouraged Britney to move to New York, where she took acting, singing and dancing lessons between attending countless auditions.

'When I'm offstage, I'm just like

everybody else.'

Britney Spears

Dynamite

It was Britney's father who sent the tape to Nancy Carson, who also represented Hollywood stars Matt Damon and Ben Affleck at the time. When she saw it, she described Britney as 'absolute dynamite' and suggested that she enrol at the Professional Performing Arts School. Shortly after, Lynne moved with her daughters to an apartment in New York.

Although many of their neighbours back in Kentwood were horrified at Lynne leaving her husband and son behind, the gamble paid off.

Money was tight at first, but Britney helped make ends meet by appearing in commercials for cars and barbecue sauce. It was not long before she won her first professional role, cast as the understudy for the lead role of Tina Denmark in the off-Broadway musical 'Ruthless!' She also reached the finals in the TV talent show *Star Search*, and in 1992 she was finally cast as a Mouseketeer alongside Jessica Simpson, Christina Aguilera, Ryan Gosling and Justin Timberlake. The following year, the Spears family moved into a Disney-owned house in Orlando, Florida.

'I feel like a totally different person than I was two years ago. I feel like so much of my innocence is gone. I'm still me, but this business makes you grow up so fast.'

Britney Spears

Step Forwards Jive Records

After *The Mickey Mouse Club* was cancelled, Britney and the rest of the family were forced to move home and return to reality. It was a tough time for the ambitious schoolgirl, and she struggled to settle back into a regular routine. Luckily, a talent scout called Larry Rudolph, who had first met Britney when she was 13, asked Lynn for a demo tape, along with some new photos. When he received the package, Rudolph was impressed and whisked her to a New Orleans studio to make a professional demo. He found six record labels that wanted to meet Britney and arranged a series of auditions; Larry would later become Britney's trusted personal manger. In June 1997, she flew to New York and belted out three Whitney Houston songs in each office. Jive Records offered her a three-month trial deal, so Britney moved back to New York, this time accompanied by Felicia Culotta, a chaperone chosen by Lynne, who remains a family friend.

'I still have my girlfriends that I grew up with. We went to day care together … we just feel comfortable with each other. We're honest, we're total goofs.'

Britney Spears

Jive's New Girl

'When I get on stage, it's kind of

like your chance to let go and be

something that you're not. It's

your time to dream.'

Britney Spears

As soon as she arrived back in Manhattan, Jive hooked Britney up with New Jersey based producer and songwriter Eric Foster White, who had already written hits for Whitney Houston and Backstreet Boys. Britney was just 15, and thrilled to be working with such a music-industry legend.

She was joined at her Upper East Side apartment by her childhood sweetheart Reg Jones and, although he supported her loyally, their romance was not to last.

Long-Distance Love

Jive was thrilled with their new signing and the 90-day get-out clause in her contract was ignored. Britney said a sad farewell to Reg as she flew to Stockholm to record her first album.

At Cheiron Studios, she met producer Max Martin, who played her a recording of himself singing '… Baby one More Time', a track he originally wrote for girl band TLC. She was talking to Reg five times a day from Sweden until his mother discovered the bill and put a stop to it. Soon afterwards Britney sent Reg a note saying: 'I'm missing you lots, but too busy to talk to you as much as I want to.'

Martin certainly demanded a lot of her time, with Britney spending 12 hours a day holed up in the studio.

'I'm a woman now, and I've had

so many cool experiences, and

awesome ones as well.'

Britney Spears

On The Brink

Britney flew back to New York with six tracks in the can, and plans for world domination. Her parents were pinning their hopes on Britney making it big, as years of financial strain meant they filed for bankruptcy in 1998, with debts of $190,000.

Britney performed a showcase of her new material for executives from Jive and the label BMG, followed by a whirlwind tour of shopping malls in a bid to reach as many teenagers as possible before '...Baby one More Time' was released in October 1998. Jive showed their commitment by giving Britney a new manager, Johnny Wright, who had launched New Kids on The Block. His plan was to create a star before anyone had even heard of Britney

Spears. Before her first single was even released, she had an album ready, and Wright had signed her up for her first tour, as the warm-up act for *NSYNC, the hottest boy band around.

'I'm not perfect; I'm human.'

Britney Spears

Heartbreaker

Britney had her first taste of public humiliation at the hands of Reg Jones, who was starting to find Britney's success harder and harder to handle. While she was recording in Sweden, Reg stayed in New York and borrowed enough money to rent a tiny apartment nearby, proudly informing Britney that he could see her window from his. But Reg was struggling to make ends meet with a part-time job as a waiter, and gradually the couple started to drift apart. When she left for the *NSYNC tour, he was heartbroken but determined to give the doomed romance one last try. When he went to see her at the *NSYNC concert in Nashville, Tennessee, he ended up getting drunk and embarrassed Britney by starting a fight. By then it was clear that Britney was moving on from her old life.

'I guess I've been under the microscope so long that I don't even pay attention to the nonsense anymore. I gave up getting upset about things people make up about me a long time ago.'

Britney Spears

Oops! She Does It Again!

'Onstage I'm the happiest person

in the world.'

Britney Spears

Thanks in large part to Jive's master plan, Britney's debut album *...Baby One More Time* sold 121,000 copies upon its release and 500,000 copies within its first month, and stayed at No. 1 for two weeks on both sides of the Atlantic; to date it has sold over 30 million copies around the world. Britney became the youngest solo performer to have a simultaneous No. 1 US album and single.

On The Road

Britney was now set on the path to stardom with hordes of fans, and levels of interest grew even more frenzied when she admitted she was dating *NSYNC pin-up Justin Timberlake. Reg had by this time packed his bags and moved back to Louisiana. Justin had taken Britney under his wing on the gruelling two-month tour at the end of 1998. It was her first time on the road and he was an old hand by comparison, as the band had by then been performing live for three years without a break.

The Spears family already knew Justin from *The Mickey Mouse Club* and, although they all liked him, they were encouraged by Jive to go along with the line that he and Britney were not dating. Britney's bosses insisted it would be easier for her to reach the top and seem more attractive to fans, if she were single. But suspicions were aroused when Justin presented her with a cake on stage to celebrate her 17th birthday. After the tour ended, Britney moved to Orlando, officially to be close to manager Johnny Wright, but by happy coincidence Justin was also living there at the time.

'I don't really have time to sit down and write. But when I think of a melody, I call up my answering machine and sing it, so I won't forget it.'

Britney Spears

Record Breaker

Almost as soon as it was released, ...*Baby One More Time* reached the top of the *Billboard* 200, then spending six non-consecutive weeks at No. 1. The promotional work had paid off but had meant a punishing schedule.

Britney made appearances on dozens of TV shows, even appearing in a wheelchair after she injured her knee rehearsing the dance routine for her second single 'Sometimes'. She was ordered to take some time out, and returned from a month's stay in Kentwood rested but with suspiciously larger breasts. After a series of sexy photo shoots she faced an outcry from disapproving Christian groups. But there were many more who wholeheartedly approved of what Britney was doing. ...*Baby One More Time* sold over 8 million copies in the US in 1999 and every magazine she appeared in sold out.

Golden Touch

Britney's bosses wasted no time releasing a follow-up, and her second album *Oops!... I Did It Again* was released in May 2000. It also debuted at No. 1 in the US, selling over 1.3 million copies in its first week of release; to date it has sold more than 20 million copies worldwide. The single, also called 'Oops!... I Did It Again', hit the top of the charts around the world and landed Britney another Grammy nomination.

The year 2000 was to prove pivotal for Britney as her 'pop princess' image was being carefully crafted to appeal to the record-buying public. Later that year Britney embarked on her first headline tour, which grossed $40.5 million. Her first book, *Heart To Heart*, was published, which her mother helped write.

Pop Princess

'So many people have asked me how I could possibly be a role model and dress like a tramp and get implants. Self-esteem is how you look at yourself and I feel good enough about myself so I wear that kind of clothing.'

Britney Spears

There was no stopping Britney. She appeared in an episode of *Sabrina The Teenage Witch*, hosted *Saturday Night Live*, and another novel, *A Mother's Gift*, was followed in November that year by her third album, *Britney*. It debuted at No. 1 and has since sold over 12 million copies worldwide. The first single 'I'm A Slave 4 U' was a worldwide hit, the second, 'overprotected', received two Grammy nominations. And in September, during a provocative performance at the MTV Video Music Awards, she ripped off her costume to reveal a barely there flesh-coloured body stocking.

But there were disappointments among the successes. Her relationship with Justin had ended and of course it was a high-profile breakup. He released 'Cry Me A River', with a video featuring a Britney lookalike, fuelling rumours that she had cheated on him.

Time Out

Further disappointments were to follow. In 2002, Britney opened a restaurant, Nyla in New York, but she pulled out within the year when she discovered the restaurant was losing her a fortune. She also had to take out a restraining order against a stalker and, after walking off stage during a disastrous concert in Mexico, Britney announced she was taking a break.

By November, she had returned to the studio and resumed centre stage in 2003, not just with her shocking kiss with Madonna at the MTV Video Music Awards, but also her fourth studio album *In The Zone*, which sold over 10 million copies worldwide.

'I do believe in the sanctity of marriage. I totally do. But I was in Vegas and it took over me and, you know, things got out of hand.'

Britney Spears

White Wedding?

She was back in business, but controversy was close by. Her private life took a fascinating turn in January 2004 when she married her childhood friend Jason Alexander at The Little White Wedding Chapel in Las Vegas. They had been celebrating the New Year with friends and, in the early hours of 3 January, they took a limo to the 24-hour chapel, which has hosted the weddings of the likes of Frank Sinatra, Demi Moore and Joan Collins. Both wearing jeans, their dawn ceremony lasted just seven minutes. The marriage was almost as short-lived. As soon as it was revealed, Larry Rudolph and Britney's manager, Johnny Wright, swung into action, in a bid to protect her $70 million fortune. By lunchtime on 5 January, the marriage was over.

'It was very upsetting and it took

a lot out of me. He was my first

real love, and I doubt I'll ever

be able to love anyone like that

ever again.'

Britney Spears on her breakup with

Justin Timberlake

New Beginnings

Britney's image was bruised, but not for long. In March 2004, she embarked on The onyx Hotel tour to promote *In The Zone*. Named after a plush hotel in Boston, where her mother had designed a Britney Spears-themed room, the tour was raking in $750,000 a night.

When the American leg of her tour ended, Britney was spotted leaving the Beverly Hills Hotel with dancer Kevin Federline. It turned out that Kevin wanted to own her heart and soul and career and, after nine years together, Britney and personal manager Larry Rudolph parted ways. Within weeks, manager Johnny Wright was no longer involved either.

Britney and Kevin were inseparable and he joined her on the European leg of her tour. In Ireland, they had matching tattoos done and were engaged by the time they came home. Plans to resume the tour were scrapped when Britney suffered an awkward fall and injured her knee while shooting the video for 'outrageous'. She underwent surgery and had to be in a thigh brace for more than six weeks, leading to the cancellation of the remainder of the tour.

'I don't want to say my biggest

mistake. Trust me I've made

plenty but I don't regret them

because they've made me the

person that I am right now.'

Britney Spears

Becoming Chaotic

'I've kissed a lot of frogs in my

life and now I have my prince.'

Britney Spears on Kevin Federline

In September 2004, Britney and Kevin gathered their friends together for an engagement party in the garden of their wedding planner, Alyson Fox. But when they arrived, even Britney's mother was surprised to learn it was actually their wedding day. The couple had been forced to cancel plans for a grand wedding with 300 guests at a luxurious beach resort after the press had got wind of it.

At the surprise nuptials, Britney wore a stunning white strapless Monique L'Huillier gown, and the brief Kabbalah ceremony was followed by a 'pimps and maids' themed bash at a Los Angeles nightclub, where the couple appeared ecstatic. The newlyweds spent their honeymoon in Kentwood and then Fiji. On their return, they splashed out on a $7.5 million mansion in a gated community in Malibu, a dream home which they hoped would allow Britney some much-needed privacy.

> *'Being married is great and I*
>
> *can't wait to start a family.'*
>
> **Britney Spears**

Prince Charming

As soon as news leaked about the wedding, rumours began to circulate that Britney was pregnant, fuelled when Kevin was spotted buying a pregnancy test in February 2005. Britney, who had already bonded with Kevin's children Kori and Kaleb, immediately gave up smoking and drinking, although the pregnancy was not confirmed until she was rushed into hospital while the couple were on holiday in Florida two months later. It was a minor scare, but the event led to Britney deciding to share the happy news with fans via her website.

Although she was on a well-earned break from recording, Britney found a new project. Her perfume Curious earned her $12 million within five weeks of its launch. Her bank balance got a further boost from a reality TV show called *Britney and Kevin – Chaotic*, which first aired in April.

A series of five episodes had been filmed during The Onyx Hotel tour, giving a behind-the-scenes insight into her romance with Kevin. The final episode, called 'Veil of Secrecy', gave a rare glimpse of a celebrity wedding. However, such a candid view of Britney's life didn't attract the viewers and the show was a ratings disaster.

'Do I know my life is weird?

It's all I've ever known.'

Britney Spears

Two Baby Boys

On 14 September 2005, Britney gave birth to her first son at the UCLA Medical Center, with Kevin by her side. They argued over a name, with Britney favouring Charlie while Kevin wanted Kevin Junior. They eventually agreed on Sean Preston, and the first photos were sold to *People* magazine for $500,000. Every move they made was with a pack of paparazzi in close pursuit, and they did not appear to be a happy family. In December Kevin checked into the Beverly Hills Hotel, followed by a trip to Las Vegas. Britney, meanwhile, sought solace at the Malibu Hindu Temple.

'I don't need Kabbalah no more

– my child is my religion.'

Britney Spears

Although they seemed to be fighting constantly and it was widely thought that their marriage was on the rocks, Britney fell pregnant again at the start of 2006.

It was a turbulent time, with the newly pregnant singer facing criticism about her abilities as a mother when she was photographed driving with four-month-old Preston on her lap. Preston was also X-rayed after falling out of his high chair. The family decamped to Hawaii, but it later emerged that Britney and Kevin had stayed at different hotels, and they were living virtually separate lives when Jayden James was born on 14 September 2006.

Little Girl Lost?

'I like meeting my fans and

signing autographs, although it

can get a bit crazy. Yesterday,

for example, a boy just came

over and planted a big kiss on

my face! I was like, "Hello?"'

Britney Spears

Less than two months after the birth of their second son, Britney filed divorce papers, citing 'irreconcilable differences' with Kevin. And while lawyers fought over custody of Preston and Jayden, Britney became a regular on the party scene with her new friends Paris Hilton and Lindsay Lohan. She was frequently photographed without underwear, clutching cigarettes and cans of energy drinks. Her life appeared totally chaotic, and although she eventually bowed to pressure and checked into the Crossroads rehab clinic, she flew back to LA after just one day.

Hair Today...

Around the same time, she stumbled into the Mondrian Hotel in Hollywood and attempted to book a room with no money or credit card, crying and saying, 'Nobody wants me anymore.' The paparazzi were on hand when she wandered into a hair salon, grabbed hair clippers and shaved off all her hair, staring wild-eyed at her own reflection. As a crowd gathered outside, Britney broke down sobbing, 'My mom is going to be so upset.'

This event that saw her so visibly distressed was seen as the most shocking incident in Britney's emotional breakdown after Kevin left.

'Why are you still taking pictures of me? Can't you see I'm crying?'

Britney Spears

Leave Me Alone

To appease her frantic parents in the wake of the head-shaving incident, Britney agreed to meet a doctor, but went out to a karaoke bar the same night. Eventually, after being urged by her former manager Larry Rudolph, her parents and even Kevin, she checked into the Promises rehab centre in Malibu, but checked out at 4 a.m. the next day and staggered into the Bel Air Hotel. Just hours later, she drove herself to Kevin's house, desperate to see her children. When photographers snapped her frantically ringing the doorbell, she flew into a rage and attacked one of their cars with an umbrella, screaming, 'Stop following me. I just want to see my kids.' Photos of Britney looking demented sold around the world. The next day she went back to Promises and stayed for several weeks.

'I don't know who to trust.

Look what happens when I

trust somebody.'

Britney Spears

Can It Get Any Worse?

Britney attempted a comeback later that year with an appearance at the MTV Video Music Awards in Las Vegas but, after a night guzzling champagne with P Diddy, her performance was widely seen as disastrous. She was nervous and unsteady on her feet, and she burst into tears the moment she left the stage.

At the same time as her custody battle with Kevin was heating up, a very vulnerable Britney was befriended by a shady character called Sam Lufti. He became her closest confidante, her manager and her life coach. She blindly allowed him to control every aspect of her life, from her career to her finances. Following damning testimonies against her in court, Britney was ordered by a judge to give up drink and drugs, and face random drug and alcohol testing twice a week. Despite the warnings, however, she continued to visit LA nightclubs night after night, and was charged with two driving offences that summer. She failed to submit to random drug tests and was caught driving without a licence, which inevitably led to her losing the children as the court granted full custody to Kevin.

'You do something wrong and you learn from it. You move on but I am having to pay for it for a really long time.'

Britney Spears

From Bottom To Top

'I'm selfish, impatient and a little insecure. I make mistakes, I am out of control and at times hard to handle. But if you can't handle me at my worst, then you sure as hell don't deserve me at my best.'

Britney Spears

It was widely assumed that Britney's new album *Blackout* would bomb in the wake of her erratic behaviour, but when the album was released in October 2007, it reached No. 2 in the *Billboard* 200 and No. 3 in the UK album charts, eventually selling more than 1.3 million copies. 'Gimme More' was also a hit, despite Britney not promoting the album at all, and music critics raved about songs that drew on her recent emotional traumas, including 'Freakshow' and 'Piece of Me'. Despite her continued professional success, Britney remained unhappy as the courts would only allow her two supervised visits a week with her children.

After one visit in January 2008, she refused to hand the children back to Kevin, and locked herself in the bathroom with Jayden. Police and lawyers were called. Britney lost visiting rights and was briefly admitted to a psychiatric ward, although she discharged herself early and drove to Mexico with her latest boyfriend Adnan Ghalib. At the end of January, police forced her back into hospital where she was held for 72 hours while doctors assessed her medical condition.

'At this point in my career I am making the music that I enjoy and the music I know my fans will love.'

Britney Spears

Daddy's Girl

Once Kevin had been granted sole custody of the children, Britney's father Jamie was granted conservatorship, allowing him to assume control of his daughter's unstable life. The first thing he did was to take out restraining orders against her shady manager Sam Lufti and boyfriend Adnan Ghalib. Jamie moved into Britney's mansion and ensured she was closely supervised at all times. He controlled not just her out-of-control spending habits and business affairs, but he also shopped and cooked for her. He created a fortress around Britney, which many say saved her life.

Experts suggested she was suffering from bipolar disorder and the new regime gave her the security and routine she badly needed. Her recovery was filmed for a revealing documentary, broadcast in late 2008, called *Britney: For The Record*, in which she admitted she should never have married Kevin: 'I married for the wrong reasons – instead of following my heart.'

'I went to a psychoanalyst. He explained things about my love life that I found almost scary. He said I had a problem with closeness and intimacy. That I was afraid of letting myself fall for someone and being hurt.'

Britney Spears

Britney's Back

In September 2008, Britney won a standing ovation when she took to the stage at the MTV Video Music Awards looking better than ever. She won three awards, including Best Female Video for 'Piece of Me' and, although she did not perform live, Larry Rudolph came back on board and hailed the start of his protégée's comeback.

'I look back and I do not see how

I got through that.'

Britney Spears

The first single from her new album, *Circus*, proved one of her most memorable. 'Womanizer' became Britney's first single to top the *Billboard* charts since '...Baby one More Time'. She performed it on the UK's *The X Factor* and, although she was criticized for lip-synching while she danced, the single sold more than 250,000 copies in the UK. *Circus* was released in December 2008, and went straight to No. 1 in the US, proving Britney was back at her best. In March 2009, just a year after she was sectioned, she embarked on a world tour and bought a new home close to where her children were living with Kevin in Calabasas.

On Tour

She was gradually gaining more access to her children. The boys travelled to London with her in June 2009 when she performed a series of sell-out concerts at the o2 arena as part of her Circus tour. Although some critics disparaged her for miming during high-energy dance routines and others for being far too raunchy for a twice-divorced mother of two, the shows were a triumph.

Mending Her Ways

'It's really weird. I've been doing this since I was 16. You could never get used to this. The best part is the fans, the fans loving you.'

Britney Spears

Britney's fans proved they were as devoted as ever by their overwhelmingly positive reaction to a special episode of the American TV show *Glee*, which paid gushing tribute to the star and in which Britney makes

several cameo appearances. In 'Britney/Brittany', Glee club member Brittany Pierce hallucinates while under anaesthetic and recreates iconic Britney moments.

Series creator Ryan Murphy said he considered Britney one of the most important female stars of the decade. The show repeated their success with a second tribute show called 'Britney 2.0.'

Britney App

Just as Madonna always managed to stay current, Britney found a new way to stay close to her fans by launching an iPhone and iPad app in November 2009. Called 'It's Britney', features included messages and news from the singer, photo galleries and Twitter updates. There was also a sparkler feature, so fans can hold up their phones at her shows and dazzle the pop star. The Be Britney's Dancer feature allowed fans to put their faces on photos of dancers and be on stage with her.

Additionally, when fans shook their phone with the Shake Shake Shake feature, they could hear Britney say, 'It's

Britney, bi***!' At the same time, she released *Britney Spears: The Singles Collection*. of course, her fans snapped it up.

> *'As the years have gone by, and as I've evolved as an artist, I've put even more into my career, and after that amount of time you start to know exactly what you want.'*

Britney Spears

Straight To The Top

In March 2011, Britney released her seventh studio album *Femme Fatale*. The lead single 'Hold It Against Me' shot straight to the top of the *Billboard* charts, becoming

Britney's fourth US No. 1 and making her only the second artist in history (after Mariah Carey) to have two consecutive singles debut at No. 1. *Femme Fatale* went on to sell 2.2 million copies worldwide, and was certified platinum. The next two singles, 'Till the World's End' and 'I Wanna Go', were also huge hits, but controversy surrounded the release of 'Criminal' because she was filmed for the video using replica guns in an area of London badly affected by riots.

A Sparkler For Britney

The year ended on a high when boyfriend and former agent Jason Trawick proposed to Britney as they celebrated his 40th birthday. After he popped the question with a Neil Lane diamond ring, she tweeted: 'oMG. Last night Jason surprised me with the one gift I've been waiting for. So So So excited!' After three years together, Jason had asked for Britney's father's permission and agreed to sign a prenuptial agreement. Although Jason stopped acting as Britney's agent seven months earlier, he has been widely credited with keeping her stable in the wake of her breakdown and turbulent romances with Sam Lufti and Adnan Ghalib.

New Best Friend, Rihanna

Eight years after Britney shocked the world by kissing Madonna on stage, it was a case of 'oops! She's done it again!' when things got heated with Rihanna as they performed Rihanna's single 'S&M' in bondage-style body suits at the *Billboard* Music Awards in Las Vegas in 2011. Britney's boyfriend Jason Trawick, who was watching from the sidelines, apparently looked delighted with the display. Britney certainly proved she was back at her best that night, showing off an incredibly toned figure. And she gained even further credibility by performing 'Til The World Ends' with rapper Nicki Minaj the same night, taking the opportunity to connect with younger fans.

When Rihanna released 'S&M' with guest vocals by Britney in January 2011, it became her tenth No. 1 single in the US, and Britney's fifth. It also topped the charts in Britain, Australia, Canada, Poland, France, Ireland and Spain.

A Femme Fatale

'The crowds have been so good

each night and that gives you

the adrenaline you need to get

through the show. It just pumps

you up.'

Britney Spears

When Britney announced plans in March 2011 to embark on her seventh concert tour, there were concerns that she may have taken on too much too soon. It did not help that within hours of making the big announcement her co-star Enrique Iglesias cancelled. However, the show went ahead, with Nicki Minaj drafted in as the opening act, and tickets sold out. Mostly featuring songs from her seventh album *Femme Fatale*, Britney included earlier hits to the delight of her fans.

As well as an homage to Marilyn Monroe, the set showed Britney as an international woman of mystery capturing a stalker and defeating a group of ninjas. She trained hard for two months not only to master the elaborate dance routines at each performance, but also to look her best in the skin-tight catsuits created for her by fashion designer Zaldy Goco.

Still Got The X Factor?

In 2012, Britney became a new judge on *The X Factor USA*, having been drafted in after the first season flopped. In a deal worth $15 million, the show's boss Simon Cowell replaced judges Paula Abdul and Nicole Scherzinger and was counting on public fascination with Britney to boost viewing figures. But once filming started, reports emerged that Britney insisted on taking breaks between every few auditions, fluffed lines and often appeared unengaged. There were also complaints that she barely looked at the teen category contestants she was mentoring while they performed, and Cowell was said to be disappointed with her on-screen presence from the start.

After weeks of speculation, Britney confirmed that she was leaving *The X Factor USA* in January 2013. *The X Factor* bosses allowed her to bow out gracefully, and Britney used her stint on the show to prove she was still a force to be reckoned with when it comes to pop music. During the show, she launched her collaboration with producer will.i.am, performing their song 'Scream & Shout'.

'No matter what you do, at the end of the day you can't please everybody. I'm not here to please.'

Britney Spears

Better Luck Next Time

After *The X Factor USA*, Britney immediately began work on her eighth studio album, *Britney Jean*, released in November 2013 through RCA Records following the disbandment of Jive Records – the label that had stuck with Britney through thick and thin.

In December 2012, she was named by *Forbes* magazine as music's top-earning woman of the year but, despite her professional success, in January 2013 Britney was nursing a broken heart again after calling off her romance with Jason Trawick. They had fallen in love when he accompanied her on the Circus world tour and, since he was 10 years older, Britney's family felt he offered her much-needed stability. But after she was spotted without her engagement ring, the couple admitted wedding plans had been abandoned. 'Jason and I have decided to call off our engagement. I'll always adore him and we will remain great friends,' she said. Jason added: 'As this chapter ends for us a new one begins. I love and cherish her and her boys and we will be close forever.'

After Britney returned his $90,000 engagement ring, Jason moved out and resigned as Britney's co-conservator. Some sources have claimed that they drifted apart over her desire to have more children; others said Jason wanted to expand his business and take on other clients - leaving less time to focus on Britney - but he did not fight for any financial settlement.

There's More To Britney. . .

'I'm from the South so I'm a very open person and I've had to teach myself not to open up to too many people.'

Britney Spears

Having been America's sweetheart for two decades, Britney has always felt under great pressure to look a certain way, but has proved she is human by occasionally allowing her weight to fluctuate, and by experimenting with different looks. In 2010, she took the extraordinary step of allowing the pre-airbrushed images from a shoot she took part in for fashion firm Candie's to be used alongside the digitally altered ones.

Her image has always been scrutinized, and many psychology experts say the defining moment in her breakdown was when she shaved off her hair, in a desperate bid to desexualize herself and escape the glamorous image that was expected of her. She apparently told salon staff at the time that she did not want anyone to touch her anymore, revealing how exhausting she found the effort of looking wholesome and conventionally sexy.

'Hand on the Bible, I know I'm not ugly but I don't see myself as a sex symbol or this goddess-attractive person at all.'

Britney Spears

Helping Others

When she first hit the big time, churchgoing Britney vowed to share her good fortune and set up The Britney Spears Foundation to use music and entertainment to help troubled kids. The Foundation supported the annual Britney Spears Camp for the Performing Arts, where children between 11 and 15 in New England, New York, Washington DC and New Orleans have the opportunity to explore their talents.

In April 2002, The Britney Spears Foundation donated $1 million to the Twin Towers Fund to support the children of the emergency services heroes who had been affected by the events of 11 September 2001. However, by 2008 it emerged that the charity was $200,000 in debt and, after Britney's affairs were passed into the hands of her father Jamie and lawyer Andrew Wallette, it was eventually closed down in 2011. She has also made donations to Artists Against AIDS Worldwide and she gave $350,000 in the wake of Hurricane Katrina. Britney has also lent her support to a number of charities including Madonna's Spirituality for Kids, Gilda's Club Worldwide, Promises Foundation and United Way.

Well Liked

As well as her apps, Britney is well known for using social media to reach out to her millions of fans worldwide (known as The Britney Army, or Britney's Bitches); she has more than 56 million followers on Twitter, making her account the fifteenth-most followed in the world, after the likes of Justin Bieber, Lady Gaga, Katy Perry, Rihanna, Barack Obama and others. As a result of her phenomenal popularity, *Forbes* ranked Britney the eleventh most powerful celebrity of 2012, in a list topped by Jennifer Lopez. The previous year, Britney hadn't even ranked in the top 100, showing just how staggering her comeback was. On Facebook, Britney has more than 41 million followers and she uses her page to update fans on personal and professional news and thoughts. Britney was also the first person to reach five million followers on the now-defunct Google+, and she has over 39 million followers on Instagram.

'I don't like defining myself, I just am.'

Britney Spears

'Every night I have to read a book, so that my mind will stop thinking about things that I stress about.'

Britney Spears

Sweet Smell Of Success

The multi-talented Miss Spears has turned her hand to a wide variety of projects since finding fame – starting in 2000 with a range of sunglasses called Shades of Britney. The following year, she landed a lucrative deal with Sketchers shoes and followed in the footsteps of her hero Michael Jackson by promoting Pepsi. In 2002, her first video game was released, *Britney's Dance Beat*, and then her fragrance Curious was an instant bestseller.

Following her triumphant return to form she was announced as the new face of Candie's clothes in March 2009, and designed a fashion line for them. At the time,

n

marketing officer Dari Marder said, 'Everybody loves a comeback and nobody's doing it better than Britney.' Another clothing partnership followed in 2014 with her Intimate Collection for Change Lingerie. Even Lidl got in on the action that year with a range of haircare products. In 2016 she launched a video game for ioS and Android called *Britney Spears: American Dream*, which enables players to 'make hit songs and climb the music charts as a Pop Star with Britney Spears!' She produced her twenty-fifth perfume, Rainbow Fantasy, in 2019, having won Hollywood Beauty Awards' Fragrance of the Year in 2018 for her 2017 fragrance Fantasy In Bloom.

Queen B

'What do you do when your life

becomes an entertainment?'

Britney Spears

Britney knew one of the best ways to prove she was back on top was to shape up. When she strutted on to the stage at the MTV Video Music Awards in 2008, there were audible gasps from the audience at how good she looked in a shimmering silver Versace dress. Gone were the wild eyes, the ill-fitting wigs and the body bloated from too much of her favourite fried chicken.

After her father moved in, and rarely left her side, she had no choice but to give up drugs and alcohol and her clean-living lifestyle was reflected in her toned new look. She was working out every day and by the time she agreed to be a judge on *The X Factor USA* she was confidently wearing a series of unforgiving body-con dresses. At the series finale, she stole the show in an elegant low-cut backless gown.

'I find it so funny that people find me so interesting. And I hate when they're like, "Define your image." I don't know what my image is. I just do my thing.'

Britney Spears

Doing It For The Boys

Britney has faced much criticism about her parenting skills, but those closest to her say she was motivated to turn her life around when she realized that she risked losing her sons.

In January 2008, cameras caught her devastation when she lost visitation rights in an emotionally charged court battle with Kevin. It was only after a restraining order was granted against Sam Lufti that Britney could begin her campaign to win back the boys. Although Kevin was formally awarded full custody, Britney's visitation rights were gradually restored and she was determined to prove she could be a good mother. She now shares custody of her children with Kevin.

On the first night of her Circus tour in New Orleans in March 2009, both sons were in the front row. She continued to provide for them beyond all expectations when her residency at Las Vegas's Planet Hollywood Resort & Casino became a blockbuster success, running from 2013 to 2017 and racking up $100 million – third only to Celine Dion and Elton John – with plans for a follow-up only thwarted by Britney taking a hiatus due to her father's ill health. Insiders have stressed how important it is to keep Britney busy, and luckily whatever temporary setbacks she may suffer, she has the potential to be well occupied.

'I think things through a little bit more, and I worry a lot. I'm more straightforward. When I was younger, I wouldn't speak up as much, but now that I'm a mom, things have changed.'

Britney Spears

On To Glory

Despite the *relatively* low-selling performance of *Britney Jean*, the single 'Work Bitch' marked Spears's highest sales debut since 2011's No. 1 'Hold It Against Me'. Her ninth studio album, *Glory*, was released in August 2016 and was included in year-end lists of best albums by various publications such as *Glamour* and *Rolling Stone*. And, her Piece of Me Tour reached the top ten of best-selling female tours of 2018.

In 2020, *Glory* was reissued amid much demand from her fans, with a deluxe edition featuring the new singles 'Swimming in the Stars' and 'Matches' – the latter being a dream-team collaboration with Backstreet Boys.

'There are so many people around you that have opinions, but you just have to listen to your instincts.'

Britney Spears

Girl To Woman

Having sold more than 150 million records worldwide, with nine bestselling albums under her belt, Britney remains one of the century's most influential and popular icons of music. She has grown up in the glare of the media, watched by a global audience of millions as she struggled to develop from an innocent schoolgirl into a sexy pop pin-up. While other child stars seem destined to descend into the grip of drug and alcohol addiction, against all the odds Britney has maintained her position as one of the top-earning musicians of all time.

A New Chapter

Although her life could never be described as normal, it seems that one of Britney's greatest ambitions is to be a good wife and mother. There was not much chance of that, given the circus that surrounded her every step of the way.

With the strict conservatorship set up in 2008, Jamie had insisted on tight regulations that gave him power over his daughter's finances, career decisions and private life. He claimed his vice-like grip was necessary because of concerns over her mental health - even when her co-conservator Andrew Wallet quit over the regulations which meant Britney could not even go on a date without permission.

For 13 years, Jamie handled every aspect of her life, even including Britney's visits to her teenage sons, and whether she was allowed to get remarried. She was dealt repeated hammer blows as she repeatedly failed to free herself from her father.

> *'You'll never see it my way,*
>
> *because you're not me.'*
>
> **Britney Spears**

When she was finally allowed to speak for herself in 2021, at an emotional hearing at The Los Angeles County Superior Court, Britney begged the judge to end the 'abusive' arrangement. Fighting back tears, the singer said she was 'traumatized' by it, adding that she had been drugged, forced to perform against her will and prevented from having more children.

And eventually, after a long running and gruelling legal wrangle, fans around the world rejoiced in November 2021 when Britney was finally released from the confines of her conservatorship when the judge agreed it was time for the star to take back control of her life. 'I think I'm gonna cry,' the star told her 35 million Instagram followers.

As a result of her moving testimony, new legislation has since been passed in the US to ensure such a strict conservatorship could not happen again.

And one thing is clear: Britney has not worked this hard or come this far to think about retiring anytime soon. Inevitably, she will continue to transform her sounds and style, and quite possibly shock us all along the way.

'For me, success is a state of mind. I feel like success isn't about conquering something, it's being happy with who you are.'

Britney Spears

Further Information

Vital Info

Birth Name: Britney Jean Spears

Birth Date: 2 December 1981

Birth Place: McComb, Mississippi, USA

Nationality: American

Height: 1.63 m (5 ft 4 in)

Hair Colour: Light brown (dyed blonde or brown)

Eye Colour: Light brown

Discography
Albums And Eps

...Baby One More Time (1999)

Oops!...I Did It Again (2000)

Britney (2001)

In The Zone (2003)

Blackout (2007)

Circus (2008)

Femme Fatale (2011)

Britney Jean (2013)

Glory (2016 and 2020)

Discography
Top 5 Singles

1998: '...Baby one More Time' (World No. 1)

1999: 'Sometimes' (UK No. 2)

'Crazy' (UK No. 5)

'Born to Make You Happy' (UK No. 1)

2000: 'Oops! I Did it Again' (UK No. 1)

'Lucky' (UK No. 5)

2001: 'I'm a Slave 4 U' (UK No. 4)

'Overprotected' (UK No. 4)

'I'm Not a Girl, Not Yet a Woman' (UK No. 2)

2003: 'Me Against the Music' (feat. Madonna; UK No. 2)

2004: 'Toxic' (UK No. 1)

'Everytime' (UK No. 1)

'My Prerogative' (UK No. 3)

2007: 'Gimme More' (UK No. 3, US No. 3)

'Piece of Me' (UK No. 2)

2008: 'Womanizer' (US No. 1, UK No. 3)

'Circus' (US No. 3)

2009: '3' (US No. 1)

2011: 'Hold It Against Me' (US No. 1)

'Till the World Ends' (US No. 3)

'S&M' (with Rihanna; US No. 1, UK No. 3)

2013: 'Scream & Shout' (with will.i.am; US & UK No. 1)

Awards (Selected)

Music Week Awards

1999: Highest Selling Singles Artist in the UK
('...Baby one More Time')

MTV Europe Music Awards

1999: Best Song ('...Baby one More Time')

Best Female Artist

Best Pop Artist

Best Breakthrough Artist

2004: Best Female Artist

2008: Best Act of 2008

Album of the Year (*Blackout*)

2010: MTV UK Greatest Track of the Decade ('Toxic')

2011: Best North American Act

MTV Video Music Awards

2008:   Best Female Video ('Piece of Me')

Best Pop Video ('Piece of Me')

Video of the Year ('Piece of Me')

2009:   MTV Video Music Awards Best Pop Video ('Womanizer')

2011:   MTV Video Music Awards Best Pop Video ('Till The World Ends')

MTV Video Music Awards Video Vanguard Award

2021:   Best Audio Mashup ('Toxic' x 'Love Shack' x Dragula remix)

Billboard Music Awards

1999:   Album Artist of the Year

Female Artist of the Year

Best New Artist of the Year

2000:   Albums Artist of the Year (*Oops! ...I Did It Again*)

Biggest One-Week Sales of an Album Ever by a Female Artist (*Oops! ...I Did It Again*)

2004: Hot Dance Sales Single of the Year ('Me Against The Music' feat. Madonna)

2009: *Billboard* Decade Chart-Topper's Top Ten Artists of The Decade (No. 8)

Billboard Year End Chart Topper

Top Female Artists of the Year (No. 5)

Top Artists of the Year (No. 7)

Billboard 200 Albums of the Year (No. 6, *Circus*)

2016: Millennium Award

BMI Awards

2000: BMI Pop Awards Honored Most Performed BMI Songs ('Sometimes')

2001: BMI Pop Awards Honored Most Performed BMI Songs ('(You Drive Me) Crazy')

Teen Choice Awards

1999: Choice Music Single

Choice Music Female Artist

2000: Choice Female Artist

2001: Choice Female Artist

2002: Choice Female Artist

2004: Choice Single ('Toxic')

Choice Music Love Song ('Everytime')

Choice Music Hook Up ('Me Against the Music')

Choice Music Female Artist

2009: Ultimate Choice Award

2015: Candie's Choice Style Icon

Grammy Awards

2005: Grammy Best Dance Recording ('Toxic')

NRJ Music Awards

2008: International Album of the Year (*Blackout*)

2009: Music Video of the Year ('Womanizer')

International Female Artist of the Year

American Music Awards

2000: American Music Awards Favorite New Pop/ Rock Artist

Music Choice Award

2016: Icon Award

People's Choice Awards

2014: Favorite Pop Artist

2016: Favorite Social Media Celebrity

2017: Favorite Pop Artist, Female Artist & Social Media Celebrity

2021: The Social Celebrity of 2021

Guinness World Records

2009: Youngest Female Artist To Have Five of Her Albums Reach No. 1 on The Music Charts

2011: Youngest Female Artist To Have Six of Her Albums Reach No. 1 on The Music Charts

Rolling Stone Magazine Awards

2001: Artist of the Year

2009: Song of the Decade ('Toxic')

Album of the Decade (*Blackout*)

Best of Las Vegas Awards

2015: Overall Show; Bachelorette Party (Britney: Piece of Me)

2016: Vegas Personality (Singer/Musician)

2017: Best Production Show (Britney: Piece of Me)

Tours

...Baby One More Time Tour:
June 1999-April 2000; North America

Oops!...I Did it Again World Tour:
June 2000-January 2001; Worldwide

Dream Within a Dream Tour:
November 2001-July 2002; Worldwide

The Onyx Hotel Tour:
March-June 2004; North America and Europe

The M + M's Tour:
May 2007; North America

The Circus Starring Britney Spears:
March-November 2009; Worldwide

Femme Fatale Tour:
June-December 2011; Worldwide

Britney Spears: Piece of Me Tour:
July-october 2018; North America and Europe

Online

britney.com:
Official website packed with information including tour dates, fan forums and an online store.

britneyspears.com:
Fan site featuring plenty of news, forums and extensive photo galleries.

@britneyspears:
Join millions of others and follow Britney's very own Twitter and Instagram updates.

facebook.com/britneyspears:
With millions of followers and hundreds of thousands of people talking about her, head to Britney's Facebook page to meet other fans and access exclusive up-to-date postings.

Biographies

Nadia Cohen (Author)

Nadia Cohen is an entertainment journalist who has worked at a number of national newspapers and magazines including *Grazia* and *The Daily Mail*. As a showbusiness correspondent she covered film festivals, premieres and award ceremonies around the world. Nadia was headhunted for the launch of a new American magazine, *In Touch Weekly*, and spent several years living and working in New York. *In Touch* now has a readership of over a million, while Nadia lives in London and juggles family life with showbiz news and gossip. Previous titles for Flame Tree include *Justin Bieber: Oh Boy!* and *One Direction: One & Only*.

Malcolm Mackenzie (Foreword)

With two decades of experience in entertainment journalism Malcolm Mackenzie knows pop culture. He successfully launched the teen magazine, *We Love Pop* in 2011, winning a BSME award for best Editor. He also launched *Oh My Vlog*, a magazine for the influencer generation to global fanfare. Between writing books on K-Pop, BTS, Friends and Ariana Grande he regularly contributes to the *Guardian*, *GQ*, *Grazia* and *Glamour*... basically anything with a 'G'.